Class and Feminism

Library of Congress Cataloging in Publication Data

Bunch, Charlotte, 1944-   comp
  Class and feminism.

    1. Women's liberation movement--United States--
Addresses, essays, lectures. 2. Social classes--
United States--Addresses, essays, lectures. I. Myron,
Nancy, 1943—   joint comp.   II. Title.
HQ1426.B84   301.44   74-13894
ISBN 0-88447-004-0

Cover photo: Smithsonian

Typeset, printed and bound by Diana Press, Inc., 12 West
25th St., Baltimore, Md. 21218. Single and bulk orders
available by mail from Diana Press.

CLASS AND FEMINISM

A Collection Of Essays From THE FURIES

edited by

Charlotte Bunch and Nancy Myron

Diana Press

Baltimore, Md.

Contents

THE LAST STRAW
Rita Mae Brown   13

GIMME SHELTER
Tasha Petersen   24

CLASS BEGINNINGS
Nancy Myron   36

SLUMMING IT IN THE MIDDLE CLASS
Ginny Berson   56

RECYCLED TRASH
Coletta Reid   64

REVOLUTION BEGINS AT HOME
Coletta Reid and Charlotte Bunch   70

GARBAGE AMONG THE TRASH
Dolores Bargowski and Coletta Reid   82

Introduction

These articles were written out of the experiences of the Furies, a lesbian/feminist collective composed of white lower, working, and middle class women. These articles reflect efforts to deal with class in the collective and as we saw it operating in the women's movement generally. They describe and talk about different class *attitudes* and behavior and are not meant to be the final statement on class and feminism in America. However, understanding class behavior among women is a useful, and perhaps essential, way to begin to understand class as a political mechanism for maintaining nor only capitalism but also patriarchy and white supremacy. More simply, class, sexism and racism.

More needs to be said about class conflict among women. The development of feminist theory about class structures in society has barely begun. This collection is one group's approach to realizing and beginning that process. Since these articles were written in 1972, we have learned more about class and women. Without going into detail, we will mention here some points for further exploration.

Class distinctions are an outgrowth of male domination and as such, not only divide women along economic lines but also serve to destroy vestiges of women's previous matriarchal strength. For example, women in peasant, agricultural, and lower class cultures are often called 'dominant' because they retain some of that matriarchal strength. Male supremacist societies must try to eliminate this female strength. The primary means of doing this both in the US and in other countries is through the domination and promotion of middle class values, including an image of the female as a passive, weak, frivolous sex object and eager consumer. The class system thus not only puts some women in a position of power over others but also weakens all women. Analyzing these and other ways that patriarchy, white supremacy, and capitalism reinforce one another is crucial to the future of feminism.

On a more immediate level, it is useful to look at how feminists have responded to the "class issue" in the past few years. At first, it "did not exist." Like most Americans, feminists believed that we lived in a classless society, with equal opportunity for all hard-working people (or at least for all worthy whites). As working and lower class women grew more conscious of being oppressed in the movement and raised the class issue, the myth was shattered. Today many feminists recognize that a class issue exists, but there is still little understanding of its significance or what to do about it. This confusion exists for lower as well as middle class women. The following observations describe some of that confusion in hopes that we can move forward faster.

The lack of class understanding in different pockets of the womens movement has caused lower and working class women to seperate and form groups and alliances among themselves. Many positive things have come out of this. Working and lower class women not only have discovered that growing up "economically deprived" is not such a bad thing and if anything they had, in fact, developed many strengths in order to survive. These strengths went unnoticed by women in a very verbal and middle class movement. Out of being together women have developed new approaches to their economic survival and have incorporated that into their survival as feminists. We can't vouch here for the number of women it has affected but we can for the overall result which is a more serious understanding of power. Understanding power starting with their own lives and applying that understanding to the systems that are in control around us.

As with any oppressed group, lower class feminists have found it often difficult to separate out which parts of oppression are positive and benifical and which are negative and self-destructive. Similarly, there are a handful of class opportunists who use real oppression as a stepping stone for personal power or a club for personal grudges. These women make it difficult for anyone to understand class issues but more important it's done at the expense of lower class women. These problems continue, but for many, greater class awareness and strength is developing out of them.

Middle and upper class women have responded to the class issue in several ways: "What, me-oppressive, I'm just a powerless woman"; downward mobility and denial of class privilege; guilt and fear; romanticizing the lower class woman, accompanied by patronization; and all too often retreat into confusion over the issue.

Recently, the primary reaction (and it is reactionary) has been to retreat from the issue and label it divisive to a feminist movement. Class is indeed divisive to feminism. So too, is race. So is lesbianism. Oppression on the basis of these differences does still prevent a real unity among women. However, they are not divisive because those on the short end of the stick begin to scream. They are divisive because the more privileged white, middle and upper class women have not recognized how they and the movement are oppressive and have not taken effective action to eliminate or at least work against class, race, and heterosexual oppression.

Working class women cannot be "blamed" for the divisions which are caused by their oppression. This is like the radical men who said women who left "their movement" to organize and fight against our own oppression were divisive. In fact, blame is not the issue. No one is to blame for the economic or class position into which she was born. The issue is what do we do with and about that position. The issue is how will we eliminate the cause of these divisions - classist behavior, class power, and class privilege - not how to shut up those who are bringing the problems out of the closet.

Some middle class women object that certain feminists are class opportunists, using the issue for personal advantage. A few lower and working class women do this just as some feminists have been female opportunists. But so what? This in no way gets the middle class woman off the hook. The issues of class are real and must be confronted no matter how someone else is using them. Class opportunists, as with all opportunists, will be stopped only when we are concretely working out class divisions among women and have a base of experience from which to stop such opportunism. Nothing short of this hard work will mitigate class conflict within the women's movement.

Another middle class cop-out on class issues has been to claim that as women we are powerless. We did not create the class system. True, women did not create class society which is patriarchal to its core. However, upper and middle class women do get privileges from that system and do behave in ways that oppress other women. As long as women support and perpetuate class divisions and privileges, we are responsible for that system, even though we did not start it. The only way women stop being responsible for class oppression is by fighting to end it.

The question for each upper and middle class woman is how to change class oppression in her life, in the movement, and the society. Behavior and privileges can be examined to see which are destructive to other women and how to change those. Skills and privileges that are gained from class connections can be used to advance all women, not just oneself or women of your class. Each woman can teach what she has gained from her class position and in turn learn from other women those strengths which she has been denied by her middle class socialization. Finally we must all work to break down the barriers of class as well as race and sexism. Barriers that are symbols of the destructive hierarchy that male culture has created to make itself feel superior.

THE LAST STRAW

rita mae brown

Now that lesbians are building a separate movement, class is a critical issue among us. Working class lesbians are determined that class will be the first issue resolved within our movement; otherwise the working class lesbians will be unable to work with middle class lesbians. Since class is so misunderstood, since it evokes such wild emotional responses, I will try to explain class in a concrete way, in terms of ideas and behavior. It would be repititious to explain class in terms of the economy--Marx has already done that for us.

America is a country reluctant to recognize class differences. The American myth crystallized is: This is the land of equal opportunity; work hard, stay in line, you'll get ahead. (Getting ahead always means money.) All public school children are fed this myth. It gives poor people hope and it reinforces middle class people's belief in their own superiority. To prove that this is the land of golden opportunity, elastic capitalism has been able to create enough tokens on many levels to keep the myth alive, i.e. the late Whitney Young, Diana Ross, Margaret Mead, etc. Visually parading the tokens promises working class people, Blacks, Chicanos, and women the chance to get ahead and channels them into the establishment where they will cut each others' throats to be capitalism's newest token. Tokenism also creates a smug security for middle class whites. It allows them to be blind to class differences by showing them the people who have "made it". The middle class person then assumes that with extra effort a "disadvantaged" person can get ahead, she just has to work harder. Since middle class people don't socialize or have close job relationships with workers there are no clashing experiences to challenge their false assumptions.

Due to America's peculiar blurring of class distinctions, middle class people do not think in class terms except for those who have become Marxist intellectuals. Middle class people often don't recognize that they are middle class. Even in the various political movements, they may recognize class intellectually but they don't understand how their personal behavior, shot through with middle class assumptions and ideas, is destructive to those of us from the working class. Even those who buy capitalism's line and want to "make it" know they are "inferior" due to class background and they work twice as hard to 'overcome' it.

Class is much more than Marx's definition of relationship to the means of production. Class involves your behavior, your basic assumptions about life, your experiences (determined by your class) validate those assumptions, how you are taught to behave, what you expect from yourself and from others, your concept of a future, how you understand problems and solve them, how you think, feel, act. (For another look at this aspect of class behavior see Nancy Myron's article, on page 35.) It is these behavioral patterns cemented in childhood that cause class conflicts in the various movements. It is these behavioral patterns that middle class women resist recognizing although they may be perfectly willing to accept class in Marxist terms, a neat trick that helps them avoid really dealing with class behavior and changing that behavior in themselves. It is these behavioral patterns which must be recognized, understood and changed.

As lesbians it is crucial that we make these changes immediately. We have few privileges in male society if we come out because we threaten male supremacy at its core. Does that mean that because we have few class/race privileges in male society that we have no class/race differences among ourselves? No. While lesbians have little power to enforce their privileges once they *come out* they still continue to behave in the ways of their class/race. It is that behavior which infuriates those of us who are not middle class and who are not white. Our anger confuses the white middle class lesbian because she can't understand what she is doing--her behavior seems natural to her.

As examples, I have singled out two ideas and their consequent behavior current in the Lesbian Movement which are harmful to working class lesbians. All too often these mistakes are deliberate stalls on the part of the middle class lesbians to keep from changing themselves. Rather than hear us, they resist us with accusations and theories to negate our demand that they change oppressive behavior.

I. THE IDEA THAT A WORKING CLASS WOMAN WITH A COLLEGE EDUCATION ESCAPES HER CLASS BACKGROUND

Middle class women theorize that if you are working class but have a college degree then you must have just as much class privilege as they do so you are no longer working class. This idea is sheer arrogant blindness. Just because many of us fought our way out of inadequate schools into the universities and became "educated" in no way removes the entire experience of our childhood and youth--working class life. A degree does not erase all that went before it. A degree simply means that you have submitted to white, male, heterosexual, middle class educational standards and passed. It doesn't mean you accept those standards. If you have a college degree you can get a better job than if you don't have one. (Unless you are a lesbian who has come out.) None of us working class women are trying to pretend we can't get better jobs with degrees than without degrees...but a job is a way to earn money in adulthood, our pasts remain the same and our ways can remain intact.

A white, middle class woman wouldn't dream of telling a Black lesbian with a college degree that she is no longer Black, yet she feels perfectly justified in telling a working class woman with a degree that she is no longer working class! There is a reason for this double think. Working class lesbians with degrees push middle class lesbians very hard. We aren't intimidated by their high tone raps and we can talk "their" language only with "our" ideas. This scares the shit out of them, many of them want to believe the class stereotype: working class people are inarticulate, shy, passive, uninterested in ideas, etc. Those of us who fight back destroy those illusions and we also destroy the middle class person's class power by doing so. The women who are the most hostile to "educated" working class women are very often, middle class women who want to cling to class behavior and the power it gives them over other women. The other middle class women usually aren't hostile, just conveniently confused, so confused that it takes them a good long time before they believe us and change their own behavior. And disbelief of a working class woman's analysis of her class oppression is one more way to undermine us--we don't "know enough" to analyze our own goddamn oppression, we need a middle class woman to do it for us in fancy sociological language. Christ.

College was culture shock to many of us from the working class. College is middle class and reinforces the white middle class woman in her class ways. College for the working class woman challenges her entire life experience. The snobbism rampant in humanities departments, the enforced practice of saying in three polysyllabic paragraphs what could be said in two short sentences are counter to working class ways. There are literally hundreds of slaps in the face that a working class woman endures. Middle class women endure the sexism of college but not the classism. Working class women get both, Third World women get it three ways. For us, college was a journey through a hostile environment, an environment where we were forced to deny our class background in order to get our degree.

College caused some working class women to reject their early lives, adopt middle class values, become upwardly mobile (or if they joined a political movement, downwardly mobile) and fight their own working class sisters to be accepted into the middle class world. Others of us endured college because we didn't want to repeat the lives of drudgery and misery our parents had, but we did not adopt middle class ways. For many of us college was the last straw that pushed us into open class resistance.

Perhaps the most outrageous aspect of the middle class women's views on education and the working class women is their unspoken assumption that we went to college because we were upwardly mobile--in other words, we wanted to be like them. Only a woman far removed from bread and butter reality could harbor such an assumption. We watched our parents slave for nothing. School seemed the answer to our economic plight if we could just get there. So we studied, got scholarships, took out loans that kept us in hock for years--to avoid that same futile labor of our parents, to survive economically rather than subsist. And in this pursuit working class women suffered more than working class men because of sex discrimination in admission and scholarships. (Plus you had to hide being a lesbian or you'd get thrown out.) In spite of all these difficulties, this generation of working class lesbians and women from 22-35 has many college graduates, a testament of grit if ever there was one. For many of us school was the first opportunity we had to have *time* to think politically. When you work all day, every day, there is little time to think and no time to politically organize. Yes, we have college degrees; no, we don't work in factories like our parents did and we learned from the rape of our parents--we want to make a revolution because of it.

II. DOWNWARD MOBILITY AS THE ROAD TO REMOVING CLASS DIFFERENCES

Youth/drug culture, the New Left, the Women's Movement and unfortunately, the Lesbian Movement are all choking on this idea. Downward mobility is a mockery of working class life. It is poverty made fashionable. Behavior remains the same: those who don't comply with this "hip" lifestyle are looked down upon. It is in the establishment of hierarchies that the middle class betrays itself--they always have to look down on somebody, a habitual attitude of power.

I don't want to live with mattresses on the floor, ragged clothes, dirt and spaghetti for supper every night. How anyone can imitate poverty and give it the flavor of "inness" is so alien to me that it is disgusting. I don't want to be above anybody but I do want decent housing, nice clothes and good food.

Downward mobility is the greatest insult yet devised by middle class people against the working class. If that alone isn't enough, downward mobility is married to the mistrust of the mind and a worship of the emotional. First of all, I don't understand intellect/emotional divisions yet millions of people seemed chained to that separation. A woman who thinks and analyzes is accused of being a power-hungry

19

'heavy' in the movement while a woman who cries at every meeting is embraced as a true sister. Many middle class women, fearing that intellect will be mistaken for middle class behavior and remembering *their* college experience, bury their brains in a morass of "vibes," "gut feelings," and outright hysteria. This is dogmatically declared "true woman" behavior since men don't express their feelings. Serious organizing to end our oppression is suspect, ideological struggle is heresy; feelings are the way, the light and the truth--even when they result in political stagnation. Such an idea spells death to real political change if people cling to it.

It isn't intellect that working class women mistrust in middle class women, it is how middle class women use their intellect to rationalize holding onto class behavior that hurts us. Or simply, we mistrust bullshit, not brains.

Difficult as it is for middle class women to realize how downward mobility strikes us, they must open themselves and see what they are doing to us. I know that for many middle class women, downward mobility was a first attempt at trying to change their ways. However, those women must realize that the irony of downward mobility, its fatal flaw, is that they could *afford* to become downwardly mobile. Their class privilege enabled them to reject materialism. For those of us who grew up without material advantages downward mobility is infuriating--here are women rejecting what we never had and can't get! Valid as that emotional reaction is on our part, we working class women are being taught a lesson by the middle class women. That lesson is: lots of capitalistic possessions and social status do not bring happiness--another American myth shattered.

One good idea behind downward mobility is non-consumerism. The problem is not the idea but how it has become part of a new middle class "hip" lifestyle, an inverse snobbism that hits working class people both ways: before downward mobility we were invisible or when visible, we were trash; with downward mobility we are "counterevolutionaries" because we don't comply with the "hip" lifestyle. It's the same old shit--middle class people develop their values and measure us by their standards and have the effrontery to be enraged if we measure them by *our* standards. Downward mobility is the other side of the capitalist coin, or to put it more bluntly, the East Village is second generation Scarsdale.

Political working class lesbians are obviously going to practice non-consumerism but we aren't creating a behavioral code out of it. We aren't trucking around in patched pants mumbling about "gettin in touch with our feelins". (Another downward mobility insult, middle class women parody our speech to prove how they are no longer middle class. This is as unforgiveable as a white person putting on a broad Black "accent").

Downward mobility also has one other dangerous effect upon those of us from the working classes--it prevents us from benefiting from the material privileges of white, middle class women. If you have money, sister, don't deny it, *share* it. If you have advanced skills don't make pottery in your loft, teach us those skills. If you have good clothes don't walk around in rags, give us some of your clothes. Downward mobility is a way to deny your material privileges to prove how "right on" you are. We know that anytime you get tired of poverty you can go right back to them (unless of course, you have publicly come out).

Downward mobility assumes that material benefits are bad. That's a mistake. Material benefits aren't bad, what's bad is that everyone doesn't have them. Downward mobility insures that working class women still won't have material benefits--we have more trouble getting them than the middle class woman and she won't share her privileges with us, she's too busy living in a dump. *Share* your material benefits.

Downward mobility and ideas centering around education are just two examples of how class can shatter alliances, make people hate each other, weaken us politically. Those examples are critical of middle class women and they deserve criticism but I'm not saying that middle class women are inevitably horrible. All I'm saying is that they have to change those ways. I am also not saying that being working class is wonderful and makes you an instant lesbian revolutionary. The fact is that there are class/race differences between lesbians and those differences have to be wiped out because they keep us apart and keep us at each others' throats. Behavior born of privilege granted from white, upper class, male heterosexuals is destructive to women and must be ended. The more privileged you were in that old world, the more you must work to free yourself from that destructiveness so that you can build the new world. But we have all lived in America and in some ways we all have to change.

In the past those of us from working class backgrounds tried to make this clear to straight sisters. We are now making it crystal clear to our middle class lesbian sisters. It is not our job to explain our oppression to you, you must work to find out how class hurts other women. Don't waste our time by trying to prove you are an exception because your father was working class and your mother was middle class. All that means is that you have a mixture of class ways; stop trying to wriggle out of those middle class ways that you *do* have. Change them. You are your own responsibility. It is your job to examine yourself and change just as it is my job to examine myself and change. Our collective responsibility as lesbians is to annilihate, smash, destroy male supremacy and build a New World.

The real question is not whether you are middle class and white but whether you are serious about destroying male supremacy, about changing the world. If you are serious you will begin by changing yourself.

GIMME SHELTER

tasha petersen

I want to talk about the youth culture and how I think it has been destructive to me and to young people in this country. The youth culture is white, male, middle class, and its values have been harmful to a political movement in this country and to the lesbian revolutionary movement in particular.

I was first introduced to "hip society" when I moved to Cambridge, Massachusetts from a rural area in New Jersey. I had grown up poor in a family of seven. I had gotten pregnant, quit high school, married young and now had a daughter. When I came to Cambridge I had had no prior contact with long-haired men, dope, bellbottoms and rock music. My thing had been drinking--anything I could whenever I could. I had read about marijuana and hippies in *Newsweek* and *Life*. I envied their "free" life but it had been far removed and romantic. I said I would never smoke grass because I didn't want to get hooked--grass, heroin, glue, it was all the same to me. Soon however, I began to feel the pressure to be "in", to be "hip". I was living with two women who had dropped out of college to work in a leather shop and who smoked dope. I soon got them to turn me on, after I had been assured that smoking grass wasn't going to destroy my brain or lead to other more harmful drugs. In time, I became part of the "youth culture".

White middle class young people going into the youth culture believe they are rejecting the middle class values they were raised with; they believe they are rejecting the role that this country has given them. For the men that role is to take over from their fathers and run this country. The men, after being trained in college, will become the lawyers, doctors, economists, senators, college professors, and the heads of big business. In short, the bright young minds of tomorrow who will keep the class system intact, capitalism on its feet, and male supremacy flourishing. The women's job is to emotionally support, encourage and give any other help necessary to keep these men and their system going. Being a wife and mother brings a woman the most reward--but these days, women, mostly white middle class women, are allowed to have a small career--as long as it helps keep the system going, and does not interfere with their husbands' careers.

The young men who say that they have rejected the role of policy-makers and caretakers of the old establishment have become the policy-makers and the ruling order of a counter-culture just as sexist, racist, classist, and capitalistic as the "old" one. The women who said they didn't want to be wives and mothers and live in suburbia are still taking care of men. Now it's "my old lady" and "my chick"--just different words that mean essentially the same thing. It's still the women who bear the main responsibility for the children. Women still get a big part of their status from the men they sleep with. This is epitomized in the "groupie". A woman has really made it big if she sleeps with a rock star, because a rock star has the most status. The more dope your boyfriend deals the more dope you have access to and the more status you have. When I was part of the male youth culture I rarely had to buy dope because there was always a man around who would supply me--as long as I would sleep with him. After tripping all night with my friends it was always me who had to take care of my daughter the next day. I never had a steady boyfriend because I couldn't stomach any man for too long a time. Because I wasn't anybody's "chick" I was supposedly open market for any man that wanted me. Whenever I turned someone down, which was pretty often, I was considered "uptight" or frigid. It was definitely uncool. In the youth culture one of the codes is sexual liberation, meaning a woman is supposed to dig fucking any man anytime, anywhere. But it's not only hip men who want to share in that liberation--I've had plenty of businessmen stop me on the street when I was looking my freakiest and ask me if they could have some of that "free love".

At first, Americans were alarmed about rejection by their children, but they soon saw that their middle class kids were not in fact rejecting their values, they were just giving them a new form. It became clear that the youth culture was not a very big threat. Why? For a few reasons: One, it upholds the basic foundation upon which all oppression is based--male supremacy kept intact through heterosexuality. Two, it's given consumerism a whole new boost. Three, drugs keep people pacified, oblivious, or "happy" enough so that they couldn't possibly carry out a revolution. Four, it certainly hasn't done anything to challenge the class system or racism in this country.

What are some of the values of the youth culture? White middle class youth know that there are more important things to life than the materialism of their parents. So they leave their comfortable homes or their parent-paid for college education and go looking for a different kind of life. This is commonly called "Finding Yourself" or searching for "soul". Through drugs, meditation, love or whatever, the youth culture tries to find the answer to the plight of humanity or the reason for their own existence. I've got news for these people, lower class people don't have to go to a maharishi to find their "soul" because sometimes that is all they've got to get through their life. I'm sure not against feeling good about yourself or trying to find some happiness but it knocks me out that people make it an occupation to the exclusion of real political work that will make the changes that are necessary for all people to feel good.

Young people coming to the youth culture are looking for freedom, but they don't stop to think that this is impossible if the world remains in the hands of those in power. In the back of their minds I think they do realize that their activities aren't going to change the world, which is why there is such a feeling of hopelessness and desperation running throughout the youth culture. This is especially evident in rock music. Freaks spend hours smoking dope, rapping, and identifying with the male rock stars who cry out in pain and disillusionment about all the ugliness they see in the world around them. But what are they doing about it? They fool themselves into thinking that if they find "meaningful relationships" with each other through love and openness that eventually the world will pick up on this and change. They will show the way for all the less fortunate people in the world.

These ideas come directly out of privilege. All their lives they have had things handed to them, have had everything they needed. Now they've created another pleasant situation for themselves, which keeps them from having to deal with the political realities of this country. They've never known what it is like to not have enough to eat--to have to go day in and day out to the same shit job because that's the only way you or your family was going to eat. If some of them have experienced being poor it is only because they have chosen the "romantic" life of poverty. The very idea of choosing poverty comes from sheer middle class arrogance and blindness to the brutalizing effects it has on people who have no choice about the way they live. They have little understanding of what it means to have to work for something, or what life is like for someone who did not come from where they came from. They left their homes and most of their possessions but they brought white middle class ideas with them.

Supposedly the youth culture is an alternate culture to the oppressive one that already exists. What are the differences? The language is different. The clothes are different. The styles are different. People smoke dope instead of drinking. People deal dope instead of working at a "straight" job. But the point is that few if any of the oppressive factors of society have changed. Women are still oppressed. Blacks are oppressed, Mexican-Americans, Asian-Americans, lesbians, the poor--they are all still oppressed--within that alternate culture.

There are still definite modes of behavior and dress that are set up as being better than others. And these are mainly oppressive to the lower class person, who like in the other culture couldn't afford to live up to them or who couldn't slip into the middle class youth culture that is not their own--whether it's hip or straight. Lower class people don't have the time to create an alternate culture for themselves--they're too busy trying to survive.

In the youth culture one of the modes is not to ever have any money. This is a new experience for white middle class people. The spiritual is "in" and material possessions are supposedly "out". Everybody says they're broke but they still have money for dope, records, motorcycles, back packs, boots, or anything else that is an accepted part of the counter culture. For many, this money comes from their middle class parents, who don't want to see their kids go without. These middle class freaks are only "broke" when it comes to the necessities of life like food, shoes, things that lower class people have to work their asses off to get. Middle class people derive status from being "hungry", while poor people worry constantly about having enough food. Freaks then wonder why working class people hate them. For a working class person who has joined the freak culture there is usually no going back. A lower class family who knows their kids smoke dope can't afford to have anything else to do with them. For the white middle class youth being busted for dope or being put down for having long hair is usually the first time they have had to deal with oppression in any form (except of course for the women who have endured sexism all their lives). For the working class person it's just the same shit all over again.

Even though they do in fact have enough to survive, white middle class freaks have now made shoplifting a cool thing to do. Never having had to take risks for survival, they create risks as tests for themselves. It's like a "gut check" to see how far you are willing to go to reject the system--how tough you are now that you're not a middle class simp. Supposedly it's the next step in rebelling against the state. But it's really a farce, because whenever any of these kids get caught they know they will not spend much, if any, time in jail. There are always "your folks" to get you off the hook, or your white middle class background--if they actually did go so far as to take you down to the station. I'm not saying we should go out of our way to pay for things we might not have to pay for, but let's not have any illusions of smashing capitalism. Nothing makes me more furious than to think that for these middle class people ripping off is a lark when there are people, mostly Black, sitting in jail because they were trying to steal some food for their kids or themselves and because they can't afford to pay the bail to get out. Bored and repulsed by the life that was set out for them by their parents, the white middle class youth has created another white middle class culture--only they've made this one more exciting.

When I became a lesbian and began to understand revolutionary politics, I began to see more clearly how drugs and the youth culture had been destructive to me and had hindered me in developing a clear analysis and strategy for changing the world. Through my lover, who is lower class too, I began to get in touch with a lot of the things I had felt but hadn't been able to understand or put into a political context. All my life I had been judging myself by white middle class male values--first in my straight life--then in the youth culture and the white male Left-- then in the white middle class anti-imperialist women's movement. I had known I was different from the middle class "freaks" I hung around with, but I still tried to live up to their standards. I was often angered at their make-believe poverty--especially when they tried to hit me for money. I couldn't stand the Left for too long because of the rampant male supremacy. Also I couldn't spout off paragraphs of theoretical abstractions.

In the women's movement I was told I didn't know about women's oppression or sisterhood because I hadn't been sitting on my ass in consciousness-raising groups talking about it for the last few years. But they included me in the "we" when they would talk about how "we" in the women's liberation movement are white middle class women and "we" have to begin to relate to lower class and Black women. Middle class people like to group lower class people together in one big unified group. They have their own stereotyped ideas of what a working class person should and shouldn't be. Because I had a fairly high political consciousness and had a father who had come from the middle class (but who kept us poor so he could "protest" the system), they couldn't see that I grew up in a lower class community and had lower class values. Lower class people are not all the same. They come from different backgrounds with different circumstances to their lives. Middle class women don't like to see this because then we would be more real to them and they might have to deal with us.

With the support of other revolutionary lesbian feminists, I have found myself--something I hadn't been able to do with three years of dope and hanging out with people who had the answer in the youth culture and in the movement. For the first time in my life I feel clear-headed, and happier and stronger than I've ever been before. I am self-identified now, no longer judging myself by male or middle class standards. Of course, none of us will ever be able to totally rid ourselves of the shit we've been fed all our lives but for me one of the biggest steps was becoming a lesbian and joining with other lesbians to begin forming an analysis and a strategy.

I had been committed to changing the conditions we live in before becoming a lesbian but I had little understanding of how. One of the steps for me in becoming more politically serious has been to give up drugs. I was smoking grass, tripping and doing a lot of speed as well as drinking. Whenever I was down, or wanted an easy high, or later when I was freaked out about what it meant to have rejected male society and be committed to women, I would do dope or get drunk. I wasted months sitting around smoking dope and "struggling".

Dope is a big part of the youth culture. People in the youth culture center their life around getting dope and smoking it. For many parts of the movement grass and psychedelics have also become a way of life. Political groups have "retreats" where they smoke dope, trip, and get their heads together". Because getting high is fun and easy, and because occasionally white middle class people get busted for it--it has become an "important" political issue for people in the movement who identify as freaks. It's a "freedom" these poor deprived people are denied. The "freedom" to get high and open up your head, to see new things and find yourself in this way, is an individual- istic freedom coming out of privilege. If we are politically serious about changing this country and destroying male supremacy, white supremacy, and capitalism, our politics have to deal with oppression that is a lot more deep-rooted than the new found white middle class oppression for being a "hippie" or a "freak". This oppression has been created by white middle class men because of their need to join the oppressed people in the world since they have some recognition that white middle class men are an enemy. But they refuse to take political responsibility for their position as oppressors of women, and they only give lip service to oppressing Third World and working class people. People of privilege must use their privilege in a way that will not oppress people of less privilege but will help those people survive physically and advance politically.

People who have made dope and long hair a sacred part of their life and an important political issue are ignoring the conditions in this country. For years heroin addiction and alcoholism have been a major problem for the lower classes, in the Black ghetto, and for homosexuals trying to survive in a straight society. Little has been done to stop this because it conveniently keeps the potential trouble-makers stupified and out of the way. Now the white middle class is flaunting dope as a whole new life-style-- just as they flaunt their make-believe poverty--a glorification of the real oppression of other people. Because middle class freaks have made dope a groovy thing to do, it has become another middle class value for working class and Black youth to live up to. But they are not coming to it from the same place or with the same privileges. Middle class freaks are trying to "get back to it all" trying to find their place with the oppressed peoples of the world. But the oppressed peoples who get into dope are escaping from a life of poverty, of scorn and hatred that they can see and feel every day, escaping from a society in which they are on the bottom. For them there is only continued but muted oppression in drugs. Dope is not a groovy thing. Dope is the enemy of oppressed peoples.

People who consider themselves "revolutionary" and

say they are serious about making a revolution have to deal seriously with the issue of dope and the apolitical values of white "youth culture". Neither dope nor youth culture can be endorsed. Fighting for these things will not bring freedom. I'm not saying there isn't beauty and energy in youth--particularly young women--but that beauty and energy is being destroyed by dope and the white, sexist, middle class youth culture. I can't take the risk of being busted for dope or having my mind spaced out/smoothed out. I get my highs from feeling clear and strong, from making love with women, from developing a strategy that is going to overthrow the present system and bring freedom for all people.

CLA// BEGINNING/

nancy myron

A revolutionary women's movement must understand the subtle yet dynamic barriers of class that exist in this advanced consumer capitalist society because class is one of the main pillars that keeps the male power system standing sturdy. Class keeps women down and divided through middle class women's oppressive behaviour towards lower class women. Instead of recognizing class for what it is, middle class women refuse to see it in order to keep many of the privileges that they get from that same class system.

Movements to date have dealt with class only in its romantic and academic Marxist sense. The romantic view of the working class is some groovy simplistic way of living rather than an oppressive product of capitalism. There's nothing cool or gutsy about being working class... it's a brutalizing and dehumanizing way to grow up. In a society responsive to images it is hard to break that romantic vision of the working class. Witness the popularity of the downwardly mobile life style.

Before we begin to figure out class and how it specifically affects our movement, we have to understand the devastating psychological effects that poverty has on the working class in this country. The conditioning and behaviour that comes from financial security and the lack of financial security are radically different. In a society based on materialism, your worth is defined by where you are on the economic ladder. One of the reasons that poverty continues in the richest country in the world is because people are brainwashed with the protestant ethic. If you're successful, it's because you work hard and are a good, clean, ambitious American. If you are poor, you haven't tried hard enough, therefore you are lazy and useless and your poverty is your punishment. The sad truth is that most poor people believe that they're inferior and act in a way that confirms it. Everything in this society keeps them thinking it. Every ad and TV show confirms their economic inferiority. Every bureaucratic insult and humiliation makes their place in society more secure in its horror. Even the material goods you acquire work against you. One can buy a color TV and car "on time", but these are visual pacifications that keep people off the streets, in debt, and even more dependent on the system.

For example, if Marsha Marvelous has nice clothes, eats good food and has a little spending money then all of her social maintenance things are taken care of. Her place is now secure in the community. If Gracie O'Neil eats boiled potatoes, Hostess Twinkies and drinks Kool Aid most of her childhood then chances are her teeth will rot out by age 15 and she will have a lousy disposition from lack of proper nutrition. And if her clothes are from the bargain table of St. Vincent De Pauls Goodwill Shop it doesn't exactly instill her with an air of graciousness and confidence as she walks down the halls of her high school. Her worth and potential in this society are questionable and at best shakey. Marsha thinks Gracie's a real frump and is that way because that's just the way things are. Gracie will usually think Marsha's better because she has a nice disposition and pretty teeth and that's just the way things are.

America has set up a scale of worth that affects everyone. If you are not white, 25, male, middle class, and do not exude an aura of virile sexuality then you are inferior. (This includes about 98% of the population.) At the top of this scale are the wealthy white males and at the bottom are the penniless powerless trash. This scale keeps everyone in line. Within it, everyone, including those near the bottom, cling to that part of their identity that makes them superior to someone else, middle class over working class, white over black, male over female, etc. And it works especially well in keeping women divided. Sexism and classism reinforce each other sometimes in outrageous ways.

For example, I moved from Boston (where I was with my own kind) to a middle class village in upstate NY when I was 12. We were the trash of the community, and were treated accordingly. I'm filled with rage when I think of what happened to one of my sisters who had the misfortune to not only be trash but to also be endowed with large breasts. She was called a whore and an easy lay. I spent much time defending her against these awful insinuations; the sad truth being that she was a shy sensitive virgin till the ripe old age of 18 when she got married. Any other woman in the village with a little financial status and the same physique as my sister was "dated" and had the respect of that foul little society. I'm not saying that the sweet magnolia blossoms of lawyer's daughters escaped sexual objectification but that they had a less traumatic time of it. Someone has to be on the bottom to hold up the top. And in this case part of the female citizenry was projected into the shadows of alleys while the rest went steady with basketball stars. It becomes clear who were the good and who were the bad. If women were stripped of these illusions of superiority they would begin to see the reality of the oppressed state of all women in this culture.

As a white lower class female, I still got one small compensation from this scale of value...racial superiority. I grew up in poverty but I had white skin privilege. Despite all my feelings of inferiority I could still "improve" my lot and even make it in the middle class. Not that I wouldn't pay for it with bits of my soul. My education, as bad as it was, wasn't as bad as a Black woman's. And as poor as we were, we still weren't as poor as the Blacks in Roxbury. I latched on to this one confirmation of my superiority with much enthusiasm.

It was only when I started to put my racism in a broader political context that I was really able to begin to deal with it. It didn't take political genius to see the similarity between the way my family was treated in the context of a middle class village and the way Blacks were treated in the context of the whole white system.

Women in our society have little control over the political system. Class privilege is one of the things given to a woman and that is given to her because she's attached to or has been attached to some male along the way (her father, boyfriend, husband) and got it from him. Most people do not deal with their racism, classism, and sexism because they accept whatever tokens of power this privileged society gives them through these systems. It is true that middle class women gain certain privileges and identity from their classism but only at the expense of lower class women. Thus they carry around a miniscule version of a larger oppressive power system. Yet because women have so little control, when you tell middle class women this, they think you're nuts. What the hell do they have to do with all that power? If you're wallowing in that shaky class security then you're not likely to admit that it exists.

There are many ways and reasons why middle class women never confront their own classism. They can intellectualize, politicize, accuse, abuse, and contribute money to in order to not deal with it. Even if they admit that class exists, they are not likely to admit that their behaviour is a product of it. They will go through every painful detail of their lives to prove to me or another working class woman that they really didn't have any privilege, that their family was exceptional, that they actually did have an uncle who worked in a factory. To ease anyone's guilt is not the point of talking about class. Some women still think that because they have a working class friend they have licked the class problem. One of the most horrifying responses in the women's movement today is that of the "political" woman who actually goes out and works in a factory so she can look at the working class women and talk to them and maybe drop a little socialism now and then. You don't get rid of oppression just by merely recognizing it. This patronization is outrageous and every woman in the place is sure to smell the stench a mile off.

Refusal to deal with class behaviour in a lesbian/feminist movement is sheer self-indulgence and leads to the downfall of our own struggle. Middle class women should look first at that scale of worth that is the class system in America. They should examine where they fit on that scale, how it affected them, and what they thought of the people below and above them. But this examination does not get middle class women off the hook; they still have to change their behaviour. Seeing your class position points out that you are not necessarily the enemy but that you too have been taken by the system. Start thinking politically about the class system and all the power systems in this country. Stop being immersed in political idealism and abstractions that have little or nothing to do with your life or anyone else's.

You are an enemy of lower class women if you continue destructive behaviour, based on your sense of middle class superiority. But you will become an ally in the feminist revolution if you will examine that behaviour and change those patterns. If women start forcing confrontation with their own class, race and heterosexual privileges, then they will both oppress other women less and begin to confront a whole system based on power and privilege. As women and as lesbians we can only count on each other to bring male supremacy down and must deal with class chauvinism before we can build a movement to make that happen.

Emily Medvic

SLUMMING IT
IN THE MIDDLE CLASS

ginny berson

The summer I was ten years old was very traumatic for my family--we had finally become so poor that we had to start eliminating basic necessities from our lives. That summer my parents had to decide between sending three of us to overnight camp at $700 a head or buying a new car to replace the other which had reached the incredible age of three. They decided to send us to camp and put off the car for another year. If the financial crisis was not real, the tension I began to feel about money was.

My father owned a children's clothing store in Fairfield, Connecticut and both my parents worked there six days and one night a week. They worked hard and were always worried about money. As I became conscious of money, I looked around me and noticed that, in comparison with my friends, and with my parents' friends, we were "poor". Most of them had two cars; we had only one. Most of them had their own bedrooms; I had to share one with my sister. Their mothers didn't work; mine did. Their fathers didn't work Saturdays; mine did. They had maids or cleaning women; we only had one occasionally. They never had to wear the same party dress twice in a row; I did.

It was more than money that made me feel "poor and deprived." It was values. My mother was always putting my father down for his "bad" table manners (burping, eating before anyone sat down, etc.). My parents had not gone to college, never read books, and didn't know anything about art. I was embarrassed to bring any friends home for dinner; I didn't want them to know how bad things were in my family. The most important attitude my parents passed on to me was that in America anyone who hadn't "made it" by this time didn't deserve to--they were lazy, stupid, or just un-American. My parents believed the American dream because it had worked for them. Their parents (my grandparents) were all immigrants who had come to the US to escape persecution as Jews in early 20th century Europe. They came to the land of the "free", worked their asses off, made a little money, and taught their children that they could and must do the same. Poverty was as much a reflection of the kind of person you were as an economic state. My parents bought the dream because they could afford to. If they were not as rich as the Joneses, they were at least richer than the Smiths. Caught in the middle, the Bersons poor-mouthed themselves because they weren't wealthy, but had the moral satisfaction of knowing they weren't poor.

The view of the world that my parents have allows for no classes. They knew there were rich people and they knew there were poor people, but the reasons for a person's economic status were personal and moral, not economic or political. Everything around me told me the same thing--America is a classless society. My high school in particular confirmed this. The tracking system started early, and by 7th grade I was in classes with people with whom I would stay all through high school. It was clearly a classist system, but the division was explained in terms of smart and dumb. The dumbs were all pretty much the same--the girls had teased hair, wore tight skirts, lots of makeup, and were considered easy lays. The boys had greasy D.A.'s, wore tight pants, were always getting suspended, and drove around the school parking lot in their hot-rods. They weren't involved in student government or varsity athletics. They took homemaking and carpentry classes. They took "business" typing, instead of "personal" typing (for the college-bound). They didn't have school spirit. The whole school was set up so that our lives would never touch. I went all the way through high school thinking they were trash because that's the way they wanted to be and thinking I was "poor" but noble because I had risen above my circumstances to be smart and clean and active.

When I was in college my political consciousness began to develop: it was the early 1960's and civil rights and poverty were in the headlines. I could both deal with my racism and get a lot of attention from my wealthy classmates with one blow--revel in my poverty. I began to see America in class terms, and put myself right near the bottom. I knew we weren't as poor as Blacks, but I was on scholarship, did have a job, and thought I had known hunger because there had been times in my family when I couldn't always have as much steak as I wanted.

By the time I left college I was very much a 1967 radical. I wanted to be an SDS organizer, but I needed money to pay back my college loans. So, as all middle class people do, I found a way out. I joined the Peace Corps--to get organizing experience, get a deferment on my loans, and learn about real poverty. (American poverty was less real than Panamanian poverty.) I would force myself to live on $120 a month, give up material possessions, eat rice and beans every day, take the bus, and live with rats, cockroaches, and poor people. I won't go into the racism and imperialism of the Peace Corps, only the classism. After a year of constant poor-mouthing to my family, friends, and Panamanian associates, I began to understand something about class and poverty. I was not really poor. I lived in a poor apartment, but I didn't have five kids and a husband to share it with. Most importantly, I knew that every month I would get paid; I knew that I could borrow money interest-free from my boss; and I knew that whenever I wanted to, I could get out. I was poor by choice, and that made all the difference in the world. And because I had economic security, I never went through the mind-fuck of figuring out how to get by from day to day.

My next phase of class consciousness started when I was back in the US living in a women's collective and working in the Women's Liberation movement. I began to identify myself as middle class, but hybrid middle class. One of the women in the collective was lower class, so I could no longer consider myself poor, but I thought I was closer to her in many ways than the middle class women whose parents went to Europe every year, who had no loans to pay back, who had never worried about money. But I never really and to deal with my middle classness until I moved into another collective where there were a number of lower class women with fairly high class consciousness.

From my point of view, being a revolutionary meant sharing everything you had, and living without whatever you didn't need (among other things). From their point of view it meant (among other things) giving up class privilege. I didn't think I had any. They wanted their own rooms; they wanted to work full time and save money; they wanted a strict financial accounting. I thought all these things were counter-revolutionary, and besides they were telling me and my middle class friends we were middle class because of the way we did things, and I thought they were wrong, so I decided class was bullshit. In the revolution there was no class. I had no understanding of where they were coming from; and it didn't matter to me that they had always been forced to share everything all their lives. They just had to struggle with that and reach the correct position. As for dealing with my privilege, I was sharing my possessions, and that should have been enough.

That house only lasted a week. We hardly knew each other, and there was no basis to trust what they were saying to me since it didn't feel right. It was only later, when *The Furies* collective formed in the spring of '71 that I began to understand that much of what they had been saying had been right. By that time I was ready to listen because I knew and trusted the lower class women in *The Furies* collective. I had reached that level of trust with them because we were agreed on our political direction--the politics of lesbian feminism.

I learned that class is not only how much money you have relative to everybody else, but what kind of economic security you have. My family never had to worry about whether we would eat, or whether my father would have work. We worried about how often we could eat at restaurants, and the kind of work my father would have to do.

For lower class women those worries are so far removed from their lives that they seem ludicrous. Eating and working are questions of survival, not taste.

Class is the way you see the rest of the world, and your place in it. Because I knew I had enough, but a little less than my friends, I was able to romanticize my "poverty". Real poverty is anything but romantic. My parents' view of poverty as a reflection of personal failure was easy for them to have because they weren't poor; for a lower class person that view is degrading, debilitating, and self-defeating. When middle class women talk about self-hate (as women), they should remember what kind of self-hate is possible when everything around you tells you that you're poor and you're trash and its your own goddamned fault.

Class is how you get educated and where. No matter how "poor" we were, there was never any question but that I (and my sisters) would go to college. I had been prepared for it by a tracking system which started early. There was no need for me to earn my own income, or help support the family. There were scholarships, and if those didn't come through, there were loans--our credit was good. Once I got to college, I didn't have to experience the culture shock many lower class women do when they step into a totally middle class world. College was just like home for me.

Class is how you act towards people. Lower class women are usually not raised in "polite society". When they are angry, they let you know it. When they have something to say to you, they say it. Glibness and indirectness are a waste of time. They don't have to spend six months in consciousness raising to get in touch with their feelings.

Class is what kinds of risks you take. Middle class women usually have something to protect. Middle class women fear the insecurity that accompanies a risk; lower class women are much less used to that security.

This is by no means the definitive article on class. Nor is it an attempt to glorify the lower class or guilt-trip the middle class. Class is a real issue which must be recognized and dealt with by middle class women without waiting for lower class women to lower the boom. I learned about class because I trusted the lower class women in our collective and because they cared about me. We have been through a long, sometimes painful process in order to get to where we are, and there are still class problems in the collective. But we are no longer blind about class.

For many middle class women the women's movement has meant a reprieve from working for somebody else's revolution. Having gotten in touch with their own oppression, they are unwilling to see themselves as oppressors again, especially as oppressors of other women. It is crucial that we stop this before our movement gets torn apart by middle class women's refusal to deal with their class privilege.

RECYCLED TRASH

coletta reid

I grew up part of the rural poor--well fed from the
garden but wearing feedsack dresses. I clearly remember
the first time I realized we were considered despicable.
We had gone to Wichita to buy new shoes for the school
year. We kids had waited for days for the annual fall trip.
Hurrying to the shoe store we passed a window with
shoes just like the ones I wanted. My parents hesitated; I
insisted. We went in and sat down five in a row. There was
no one else in the store. The clerks continued their light-
hearted and easy chatting. No one noticed us. As we sat
there waiting, a feeling of dread began to grow on me.
Finally my father mustered his dignity and marched us all
out leaving the hypocritically apologetic clerks behind.
Outwardly we were righteously indignant; underneath we
were all properly humiliated. None of us ever mentioned it

again, but I knew without asking: everything about us was wrong--the way we looked, talked, dressed and moved.

My grandfather was a farmer, my father a self-taught mechanic who worked on farm machinery. His cinder-block garage was only thirty yards from our house; next to it were junked cars and piles of pipe and scrap metal. When I was four my mother quit her job as a storeclerk. She spent all her time raising the garden, making our clothes, and helping in the garage. When I was ten she went back to work, this time in the post office. Soon we got a used piano and I began lessons. Then a TV, and finally my father's dream: a red accordion so someday I could be a woman accordionist on the Lawrence Welk show.

After I started high school in town I realized that the attitude of those Wichita store clerks was shared by most people. In my one-room country grade school we were all pretty much alike--dirt farmers' kids. But in town there were professionals' kids and businessmen's kids and a pecking order with us on the bottom. Everything in town belonged to that order: what church you went to, which stores you shopped at, where you spent your lunch hour. During my freshman year I had a crush on a farm boy-- dirty fingernails, workboots and all. I never got up enough courage to do more than ride around in his old car after school, but soon I heard around school that I was "easy." I spent the next three years living down a reputation for looseness. All of us poor farm girls had to prove we were moral, while it was assumed of the businessmen's daughters. From then on I waited for a nice clean professional's son-- someone to confer status and respectability on me.

My parents were what my middle-class sisters so scorn-fully refer to as "upwardly mobile." I guess that means that they didn't want me to be treated like dirt all my life like they had been. There were two things my mother drummed into me: get an education and stay away from boys. She saw education as the way out, the one thing that guaranteed financial security and respect. Men were the stumbling block to that goal. They got you pregnant and left you or got you pregnant and married you to a lifetime of low-paying jobs and housework. She had wanted to be a bookkeeper but had had to go to work right after high school to help support her family. After getting married she still had to support the family but had to cook and can and clean too. She wanted me to get married, but only after I had gotten the education to be able to do what I wanted to.

On scholarship, I went to a little fundamentalist church college in Oklahoma. There I began a long apprenticeship in the art of appearing middle class. I improved my grammar, increased my vocabulary, learned about classical music. College initiated me into an alien culture that I knew I had to master to go anywhere. From the first week on I stood demurely chatting and sipped hot tea, took showers and acted like I felt right at home in long-winded academic discussions. I found out that there were hundreds of books everybody else could discuss that I hadn't even heard of. I went to college so I wouldn't always be a waitress or nurses' aid, getting the smallest salary for the heaviest work in the place. But I found that college doesn't just prepare you for an easier, better-paying job; it insures that you dress, talk, and think like a member of the professional class--that includes thinking you're better than working-class people and their culture.

Evidently I had learned my lessons well because I was rewarded my junior year by marriage to a doctor's son. I entered a family smug with the security of its social position. Rooms lined with books, a stereo, rolled roasts, asparagus, coctail parties. In one dizzying stroke I went from drive-in movies with a Dairy Queen afterwards, to symphony concerts and late Chinese dinners. The next two years were the unhappiest ones of my life. Somehow I had believed that middle-class marriage would be different from working-class marriage. My father had been a total authoritarian patriarch; our family had revolved around him and his wishes. Whenever we got out of line we were brutally brought back. Just two weeks before my wedding he beat me for doing something he didn't like. But I thought that in middle-class marriages women would be equal to men. My mother-in-law was even a poet and painter. Violence was unheard of. It took a while but I learned there was only a difference in style not in substance. My husband never hit me; he just got up in the middle of the night and went for a walk. After I anxiously waited for hours for him, he came home, having decided not to hop the next train out of town. The message came through loud and clear. Stay in line or your emotional and financial security will disappear without so much as a good-by.

While I was still married I fell in love with a woman who was *upper* middle class. She was everything I was not. She could have met the Queen of England without batting an eyelash. Sure of herself and her place, she accepted my devotion carelessly as if it were her due. I was only too happy to be allowed near her, to have other people know I was her friend. I secretly hoped that her beauty, confidence, and ease would rub off onto my drab self. I moved into a women's commune with her thinking I was middle class like most everyone else. I had been to college; my husband had been a professional. But it was soon clear that the experiences and outlook of women whose parents had been well off were very different from mine. As they sat and joked about their "moms" I tried to imagine being pals with my mother. When they went shoplifting at Lord and Taylor I couldn't imagine being comfortable enough even to go in. Just like old times I felt on the outside of the "right" experience.

I have spent most of my life wanting to be part of that right experience. Since I have been in a lesbian/feminist collective I have started looking at where I came from, where I got to, and what happened to me along the way. When other working-class women started confronting oppressive middle-class behavior I sat on the sidelines and listened. I didn't want to risk the little respect from others that I had built up since being in the movement. I didn't understand why working-class women had to be so hostile; I understood and agreed with what they were saying but I couldn't understand why they insisted that others change. Because I had been accommodating for years it seemed only natural to me. But I finally had to choose whether to align myself with those who came from backgrounds like mine or with those I had been trying to emulate. I saw that choosing to risk the favor of my middle-class friends was choosing myself. To stop accommodating hasn't been the only pattern I've had to change; I've also had to question all those middle-class attitudes I'd accepted to find out which ones were worthwhile and which ones oppressive.

The most oppressive attitude I had accepted was that because I had become middle class, worked my way "up," I was better than other working-class women who were still down there. I had gone to college; if they had been as smart as I was, they would have gone too. It was partially their own fault that now middle-class women still treated them with disrespect. When other working-class women challenged my attitude, I felt like life had been particularly unfair to me. I had spent years enduring the disrespect of others and proving myself worthy and now I was being punished for it. I had taken one of the survival roads open to me and now I had to stop surviving that way.

There are many of us "upwardly mobile" lesbians in the movement--women whose college educations weren't a privilege, who fought every step of the way to get where we are, who are now less class oppressed than we ever have·been. But we are only less oppressed because we have become more and more like our middle-class sisters. It is crucial to dealing with classism in our movement that we start throwing our lot in with our less "upwardly mobile" working-class sisters and start questioning our own middle-class attitudes and ways of behaving. We may have had to learn those ways to survive, but they're not helpful now in building a movement aimed at changing society.

REVOLUTION BEGINS AT HOME

coletta reid &
charlotte bunch

Early in the Women's Liberation Movement, I saw class as an "issue" that men in the Left used to put down feminism. Later it became an "issue" that many women said we had to discuss, but these discussions never went beyond wondering why welfare mothers weren't beating down our doors. Hours were spent beating breasts with guilt. The verdict: Women's Liberation was middle class and that's bad, but we never understood why. We never examined how our behavior created and perpetuated that kind of movement. We never looked at how working class women within our movement were oppressed.

When class became an "issue" in the development of a lesbian feminist movement in D.C., I was apprehensive. Academically, I knew that class divisions existed and ought to be abolished, but I did not connect that to my behavior or to what was happening to women in the movement. Of course, I did not imagine that I was a class supremacist. Only after months of struggle (or should I say, fights, hostility, withdrawal, trauma...) did I begin to understand that much of my behavior came from being raised middle class and was oppressive to working class women.

I finally recognized that class in our society is not only an economic system that determines everyone's place, but also patterns of behavior that go with and reflect one's status. When middle class women carry their attitudes and ways of behaving into the movement, it oppresses working class women. Class divisions and behavior come from male dominated society and it is absurd for us to perpetuate them. If middle class women remain tied to male class values and behavior, we cripple our growth and hinder the development of a movement that can free all women. Class struggle is not a question of guilt--it is a question of change, for our movement's survival.

I come from a thoroughly middle class family (economic security, education, etc.). Coletta comes from a working class home, worked her way "up" through college and a "good marriage" and accepted middle class values that oppress working class women. From our experiences, we will describe ways that middle class women are oppressive, how we avoid class consciousness and changing ourselves, and how we must change.

Classist behavior is rooted in one basic idea: class supremacy--that the indivduals of the upper and middle classes are superior to those of the lower classes. Middle class people are taught to think that we are better than working class people and we act out that superiority and self-righteousness in a thousand daily ways. Class supremacy, male supremacy, white supremacy--it's all the same game. If you're on top of someone, the society tells you that you are better. It gives you access to its privileges and security, and it works both to keep you on top and to keep you thinking that you deserve to be there. It tells you over and over that the middle class way is the right way and teaches you how to keep that way on top--to control people and situations for your benefit. No one in our movement would say that she believes that she is better than her working class sisters, yet her behavior says it over and over again.

Class supremacy is acted out in thinking that working class women are less together, personally and politically, because they do not act and talk the way we do. Their politics may not be expressed in the same manner, their vocabulary may not be as "developed", and so they are "less articulate" and treated as less important. Or they may be hostile and emotional so one can hardly trust their political judgement; after all, we've learned to keep ourselves in check, to be reasonable, to keep things in perspective. Looking down with scorn or pity at those whose emotions are not repressed or who can't rap out abstract theories in thirty seconds flat reeks of our class arrogance and self-righteousness.

Other middle class women pull the opposite number: emotionalism, hysteria and tears when you're feeling bad and things don't go your way, or begging sympathy because it's just to hard to change. To a working class woman this constant preoccupation with one's feelings and the difficulty of changing is a luxury she could never afford. She is tired of hearing how it's really hard for you to change because your mother was neurotic, etc. while you go on oppressing her. She had to do many unpleasant things that middle class women complain about endlessly, like exploitative jobs, just to survive. Endlessly analyzing and discussing your feelings is another way to keep control, which involves both out-talking people and using your feelings as excuses.

Sometimes a middle class woman feels superior because she believes that she worked for what she has--that her skills, education, possessions and position--come, not from her class privilege, but from hard work. I used to feel this way because I compared myself to the rich, not the poor; so, I thought that I did not have a lot to start with and had earned what I did have. By downplaying the role that privilege played in getting each of us to where we are now, we can keep on thinking that anyone can make it if they "try as hard as we did."

For example, I used to think that I had savings because of my good planning and frugality. Although I had saved a lot at a low salary, I was not recognizing that my ability to save came from my privilege--that I had inherited economic security and actual possessions to afford to live cheaply. If you think that you are where you are just because you worked hard, it is easy to become self-righteous and make classist moral judgements about others.

Often, middle and especially upper middle class women for whom things have come easily develop a privileged passivity. Someone with privilege can conveniently think that it's not necessary to fight or discipline herself to get anything. Everything will work out. Because she has made it by following nice middle class rules of life, she doesn't like for people to be pushy, dogmatic, hostile, or intolerant. Material oppression doesn't bombard her daily, so she has the luxury and time to move slowly and may resist taking a hard political stand or alienating "anyone." She can afford to assume that most people are good and that it is unnecessary to fight or prove oneself to anyone.

Advocating downward mobility and putting down those who don't groove on it is another form of middle class arrogance. Someone who has never had to worry about eating or being acceptable can leave a job easily without knowing where money will come from, embrace patched pants and brown rice and anti-materialism as good for the soul, and treat with disdain those who are hung-up with material needs. She can usually also go back to her parents, college, or a good job when she tires of poverty. Once more, middle class women set the standards of what is good (and even the proper style of downward mobility which often takes money to achieve) and act "more revolutionary than thou" towards those who are concerned about money and the future. Often these middle class revolutionaries then live off of working class women, who haven't discarded all their property (which the middle class women may carelessly destroy) or who keep their jobs because of the fear of real poverty. This sharing is done as "revolutionary communism," but since it ignores the different class realities of those involved, it is a fuck over.

The "more revolutionary than thou" attitude is only matched in arrogance by the paternalistic social worker type who understands the "problems" of the working class woman and wants to help her out. Psychological paternalism occurs when one middle class woman explains to another that "you have to understand Mary's background and why she is so hostile." What Mary needs is for her to stand up and fight classist behavior with her not explain away why she is the way she is. Paternalism can be benevolence in which the middle class woman gives out of personal graciousness, rather than from the recognition that she has class privileges which it is her responsibility to share. She also retains control over the access to privilege and withdraws it when she disapproves, i.e., when she is threatened. Whatever form the behavior takes, it is condescending because it assumes class superiority instead of recognizing that as women raised in the middle class we have recieved some useful benefits (such as money, education, skills) which we can share. It is arrogant because it accepts society's idea that privilege makes you better when, in fact, being raised middle class has messed us up in many ways which working class women can help us understand and change.

There are a lot of small, indirect, and dishonest ways of behaving that are part of being raised in "polite society" where "being nice" is at a premium. One is being indirect about anger and disapproval in destructive ways: we bitch, harp, withdraw, make snide comments, gossip, pout, etc. We make people feel our disapproval or anger but we do not say what is really on our minds.

Some of us try to smooth things over and prevent open conflict which we fear. I did this because I took conflict and anger personally and assumed that if the other person liked me, she wouldn't get angry. It was hard for me to get over an angry scene, so I tried to avoid hostility. This behavior gives the illusion that things are o.k., that you're still under control, but it is dishonest and destructive because it does not resolve problems and messes over the person who is direct about her opinions and feelings.

These are only some of the forms of classist behavior

that we have come to understand in our group. No one woman has all of these traits. On the surface many of these forms seem opposite or contradictory, but what is important is that they are all ways of maintaining the supremacy of the middle class and perpetuating the feelings of inadequacy of the working class. We are not saying that all middle class values and traits are inherently bad; many are helpful and when disassociated from supremacist use can help us all. But if we are to be able to use any of these and to develop new non-classist ways of behaving, we must examine the effects of our present behavior and how we resist changing.

RESISTANCES TO CHANGE

When working class women start confronting middle class women with their oppressive attitudes and behavior, they begin to hear a series of defenses and rationalizations that would stagger a horse. It is not helpful to defend ourselves when someone tries to point out our classist behavior. It is important to be as open as possible, to listen to the working class woman and change what she tells us. Working class women don't confront us because they get their kicks that way, but because they want to work in a movement with us and they can't do it unless we stop oppressing them.

The following are some of the ways middle class women react when confronted. None of them are helpful. If you find yourself acting in these ways, stop.

First, there are several ways to divert the issue and avoid dealing with criticism. A common diversion is denying that we are *really* middle class. Our father worked his way up, or we come from a "hybrid" family, or all those definitions of middle class don't really apply to us. Of course, this in no way deals with what the working class woman is saying to us about our class supremacist behavior.

Or we deny that the woman criticizing us is *really* working class. She may have gone to college, or she dresses "well", or she's as articulate as we are. Anything to throw into question her criticism of us. According to this diversionary tactic, only a woman with six kids working in a factory can say anything to us about our class oppressiveness.

It is also diversionary to accuse the working class woman of denying our oppression. She's not denying that we are oppressed as women. All she is saying is that we also oppress her because of our class supremacist behavior.

Then we can always avoid the issue by demanding to know how working class women are going to bring about an economic revolution. When they start talking about our class oppressiveness, we start inquiring about their program. How will our being unoppressive help the coal miner's wife? What are they doing to alleviate the plight of Peruvian Indian women? Of course, the point of our changing is to build a movement together aimed at changing the condition of all women.

The second most common way of dealing with class criticism is the guilt trip. The purpose of criticism is to make us change not to make us feel guilty. It's not our fault that we were born middle class and breast beating about who our parents were and how we grew up isn't helpful. It is our fault, if after being told how we're oppressive, we just feel bad and guilty but continue the same oppressive behavior. Guilt makes us know we ought to be "concerned" about working class women so we add them onto the end of statements or talk about how we ought

to have more articles about "them." Guilt is not a helpful way to react to someone pointing out our class supremacist attitudes and behavior. It's just another way of
not changing.

One of the most common ways of expressing guilt
is to glorify the lives of women who were raised in working class homes. We talk a lot about "far out working
class dykes" and wish that we hadn't been raised in the
suburbs. This in no way deals with the economic insecurity and position of inferiority that working class women
grew up in. It's pretty upsetting for a working class woman to look back at her own life and how she has been
treated like scum, while we are telling her what an exciting experience it must have been. Then there are middle
class women who put working class women on a pedestal
to admire, imitate, or observe with delight. This is just
another way of denying that working class women are our
equals to be listened to and struggled with.

A step up from out right defensiveness and guilt occurs
when middle class women begin to realize the force of
criticism but are unable to deal with it politically. So
we take it personally. We talk and feel as if we are being
unjustly attacked, as if the other woman has no real class
grievances against us but is just hostile. "Nowadays, she's
just angry at me." Instead of looking at our behavior
searching for anything that might be class supremacist,
we assume the working class woman is being unfair to us
for no reason. Generally, instead of seeking her out to
find out what's wrong, we withdraw in confused "hurt"
thereby protecting our classist behavior. Often we feel
self-righteous because she's the hostile one. "I tried to
keep up the friendship, but she just wasn't open."

Once we have a little class consciousness we don't

think that the working class woman is being unfair for no reason, but we think she has things out of perspective. Her hostility is greater than our oppressiveness warrants. We feel as if we are scapegoats, as if all her hostility from every source is directed at us. She has everything out of proportion and how can we change in such an environment?

Often middle class women react as if working class women want to take away our very identity. "They don't want us to be ourselves; they can't accept strengthsin anybody." We don't know if any of our behavior is any good anymore. So we become totally passive and of no use to anyone. We acceptingly listen to all criticism with apparent openness and understanding. Yet, we do nothing. Our "polite" acceptance is a passive evasion. If directly challenged, we say, "You're right but I can't deal with that now." We don't take initiative because it might be classist. This sort of passive withdrawal from the fray is a very effective way of not having to change. It indicates that we know that part of our identity is based on our middle class ways of acting. Middle class women have to build identities that are not based on our supposed superiority. The way the system has worked we have built who we are partly on whom we are better than.

Another passive reaction to class criticism goes, "Yes, I know I'm classist, and I really need you to struggle with me. Tell me every time I oppress you and I'll change."

This puts the responsibility for change back on the working class woman. We are the ones who are oppressive, so it is our responsibility to search our own and other middle class women's behavior and attitudes and to respond openly to working class women when they confront us.

We have to trust that working class women aren't just trying to tear us down, that they want us to change, that they value us as persons apart from our class oppressiveness. For sure, working class women don't struggle with those they don't care about or who they don't think will change. We can't wait for someone else to make it clearcut, totally explained and unambiguous. If part of what someone says about us seems wrong, we shouldn't use that as an excuse to dismiss it all. We have to examine ourselves, what others say and learn by risking change.

The anger of working class women towards middle class women is justified by life-long class oppression, and the class system will not be changed until middle class and working class women *both* see how oppressive it is and unite to change it. Working class women want middle class women to take up the struggle against classist behavior as their own, to stop resting on their secure middle class position. Middle class women haven't had to make the fight against classism important because we got benefits from it. We were in the superior position. Working class women want us to stop supporting the class system by accepting its middle class values, stop resting on our privileges and start confronting and challenging class oppressive behavior in ourselves and other middle class women. They do not want to be the only ones who fight against classist behavior. If they are, they might as well separate into their own movement.

Working class women also want us to use and share our middle class privileges with them--the things and skills we have because we were born into the middle class. They want us to share our money, our property, our access to jobs, our education, and our skills. Many middle class women think that downward mobility (voluntary poverty) makes them less classist. In fact all it makes us is poorer and unable to share potentially large salaries with those who don't have the choice of voluntary poverty.

Bringing down the male supremacist system in this country will not be a possibility until we stop acting out our class supremacist attitudes on the women with whom we're building a movement.

GARBAGE AMONG THE TRASH

dolores bargowski & coletta reid

Lots of us in the Lesbian/Feminist Movement come from lower and working class backgrounds. It's not true that all of us are middle-class; it's just that the middle-class women have run the show. Middle-class ways of doing things are the standard. Those of us who are lower or working class have gone along with and been successfully divided by middle-class dominance. We have often tried to stop their dominance but middle-class lesbians--because of their larger numbers, power, and privileges--have kept us divided. The following skit shows how one middle-class lesbian (Garbage) can keep two lower (Trash) and working-class (Goodie Goodie) lesbains separated from each other and maintain her control.

Garbage: (To Goodie Goodie) Pass the chicken, will you please? Thank you. (MEANING: Garbage sets the polite tone of the dinner.)

Goodie Goodie: You're welcome. (MEANING: Goodie Goodie's gonna play the game.)

Garbage: (To Trash) I saw Peggy today. She said you were in the bar last night.

Trash: Yeh, me and Peggy had a couple beers together and talked about the old days. We had a real nice time.

Garbage: I thought you were low on money. That's why I gave you that ten dollars.

Trash: I am.

Garbage: Well, if I'm going to give you money I don't think you should be spending it on beer. (MEANING: I can make better decisions than you can.)

Trash: (Gulp. Silence. Defensively.) Well, I didn't spend that much in the bar. I only bought two beers. Anyway, what are you complaining about, you went out to dinner twice last week. (MEANING: Shit, fuck, piss, next time it'll be harder than hell to borrow any money from her.)

Garbage: (Taking advantage of Trash's defensive position, instructs her in the right values.) Why don't you spend your money on useful things? Or save it so you can buy that camera you want. (MEANING: If she'd only use her head like me and be more responsible with her money she'd get what she wants. I just don't understand what her problem is.)

Goodie Goodie: When I was in High School and my family didn't have enough money to buy me a car, I saved for two years to get one. (MEANING: I worked my way up to be like Garbage. See how I've improved. You could to.)

Trash: (Laughs.) What'd you use for gas money? Your savings account book (MEANING: Hostility.)

Goodie Goodie: (Shot down and angered.)

Garbage: That's not funny. (MEANING: Why aren't you more grateful?)

Goodie Goodie: Garbage works hard for her money. She's been riding the bus to work for months. (MEANING: Garbage works hard for her money and you don't. She sacrifices for you. She's wonderful and so good to ride the bus cause it's beneath her to do it.)

Garbage: (Feeling fired up by the support from Goodie Goodie, speaks from her throne angrily.) Don't you see I'm just trying to help you. (MEANING: I know what's best for you better than you do. What's best for me is what's best. I am right. You're wrong.)

Trash: (Intimidated by Garbage's fierce sense of rightness and Goodie Goodie's sympathy and support of Garbage.) I guess you're right. (MEANING: Anyway, they're both against me, so I'd better keep quiet and go along with them.)

THINGS LEFT UNSAID BY TRASH

Oh, I'm so hungry. I wish I could just grab a chicken leg. I guess I'd better wait 'til everybody's served. I wonder what I should talk about now. Garbage looks like she has something on her mind. I wonder what it is. So that's it, money again. Christ. What's wrong with beer, anyway? I'm not an alcoholic. I wish she wouldn't bring this up in front of Goodie Goodie. Garbage doesn't like beer. Maybe I should drink Manhattans. But I like beer. I really don't spend that much on the bar. I only went once last week. She went out to dinner twice, probably spent a lot more money than I did. Oh, shit, I shouldn't have brought up about the dinners. She's right, though, I do want a camera. I just don't know how to manage money very well. Even Goodie Goodie knows how to manage money better than I do. But shit, I wish she'd stop rubbing it in. I feel like kicking her in the ass. Ha! "What'd you use for gas money? Your savings account book." Oh, she doesn't think that's funny. Why am I always putting my foot in my mouth? Somehow I never do anything right. I wish I was more together. It'd make it a lot easier. She seems to be able to handle anything. She'd probably already have that camera. Maybe I really don't want it. It's probably my own fault. Sometimes I think I'm hopeless. If I'd save like they say I should maybe I'd get it. She really is only trying to help me; I like her too. "Yeah, I guess you're right." But I really feel down.

This skit is an example of what happens when lower and working class women still accept the middle-class standard. The middle class (Garbage) sets the tone and controls the conversation. Trash is put on the defensive. She feels like she has to explain and justify her actions. She starts out feeling something is wrong with what Garbage and Goodie Goodie are saying, but she ends up feeling like she's wrong.

She begins to doubt herself and feel like nothing she does is worth anything. Then she starts getting angry at herself. Trash doesn't get any support from Goodie Goodie who keeps running to Garbage's aid. Goodie Goodie has a stake in Garbage's staying on top. She gets approval and status from being with Garbage. She doesn't really believe that Trash could support her as well as Garbage does. She wants the approval of the middle class, not of someone who's close to where she came from, because she's constantly reminded by the middle class that where she came from was no good.

We've been in lots of situations like this skit. It doesn't have to be around money or beer. Anytime middle class lesbians have the power and we're fitting in or identifying with it for survival, the same sort of thing happens. We come off feeling like shit and feeling weak and unsupported. We end up further supporting middle class dominance and the lie that we are nothing on our own without the middle class.

We have found that there are specific things that keep us in this position. They work to undermine, make us feel guilty and strip us of the confidence we do have. The next skit includes some of these ways, but rather than going along with them, the lower and working class lesbians challenge Garbage's control. They've stopped believing she's right because she's middle class.

Garbage: (To Goodie Goodie) Pass the chicken, will you please? Thank you. (MEANING: Garbage sets the polite tone of the dinner.)

Goodie Goodie: You're welcome. (MEANING: Goodie Goodie's gonna play the game.)

Garbage: (To Trash) I saw Peggy today. She said you were in the bar last night.

Trash: Yeh, me and Peggy had a couple beers together and talked about the old days. We had a real nice time.

Garbage: I thought you were low on money. That's why I gave you that ten dollars.

Trash: I am.

Garbage: Well, if I'm going to give you money I don't think you should be spending it on beer. (MEANING: I can make better decisions than you can.)

Trash: (Gulp. Silence. Anger.) Beer is good for your health, and it's full of B vitamins. (MEANING: Who's she to say what's good for me. Just because she gives me a little money she thinks she can control what I do.)

Garbage: You're missing the whole point. (MEANING: You're stupid because you can't follow my reasoning. It's my money and I should have a right to say how it's spent.)

Trash: The whole point is that you gave me the money but you want me to get your stamp of approval before I spend it. You want me to jump when you holler. You want me to kiss your ass and act like a proper beggar.

Goodie Goodie: (To Trash) You're behaving like a bar room hussy. Let's be rational about this. There's no reason to argue. Let's talk about it calmly or we won't get anywhere. (MEANING: Trash, your behaviour is out of line. Garbage's way of talking things over is the right way to work things out.)

Trash: (To Goodie Goodie, angrily) Listen you ass-kisser chicken-shit fart. How many times did you tell me the story of when you were a kid and cashed in your parents' empty beer bottles to get money. You've got the gall to call me a bar room hussy when you drink a glass of wine at every dinner. You're just playing up to Garbage so she'll pat you on the head and throw you a scrap of approval. (MEANING: You're not so superior. You're not so far away from trash yourself.)

Goodie Goodie: (Gulps. Squirms.)

Garbage: This is getting foolish. (MEANING: This is getting out of my control.) I only brought it up because I knew you were trying to save for a camera. I just wondered how it was going. (MEANING: I am pretending concern for you to disguise the fact that I have a right to say where the money's going.)

Trash: (Taken aback) Well, I was going to start putting my money away. (MEANING: Yeah, I really want to get that camera) but... (MEANING: Wait a minute, what is this shit?) What the fuck difference does it make? If I want a camera, I'll get it somehow. You think your way is the only right way. Get off my back will you.

Goodie Goodie: Wait a minute. Let's stop this right here. I'm not sure how this has all happened, but it's gotten to be a mess with me and Trash fighting on each other. I'm sure Trash will get the camera. (To Garbage) And she doesn't have to give you a detailed account of her actions to get it. What's the camera got to do with this anyhow, or a few beers for that matter.

Garbage: (To Goodie Goodie) I'm surprised at you. (MEANING: How come you're not supporting me?) I've always hoped we could rely on each other. (MEANING: Divide and Conquer. I respect you more than Trash. You are better. I'll even give you the support you need if you will keep supporting my control.)

Goodie Goodie: (confused, angered and somewhat speechless) (To Garbage.) No. Stop this shit. Whenever you tell me how good I am I start expecting it from you. I stop believing in myself and look to you for what I know I already have. I feel like I have to keep behaving then so you won't take your support away. You make me dependent on you when I don't need to be. You make me pay for the support you give to me. I'm through giving you the power to punish me if I step out of line. Do you hear me.

Garbage: (sitting motionless with a stone face) I don't know what you're talking about. (MEANING: I wish to cancel out everything you've said. I refuse to listen to you. Right now you're too threatening to me.)

Goodie Goodie: Well, I'm not surprised. I doubt if you ever really listen to me except when it's something useful to you.

Trash: (To Goodie Goodie) My God. You're really something. I thought you had guts underneath you but I didn't know what was stopping you up.

Goodie Goodie: I guess I'm just fed up with trying to meet someone else's standard. Always being told you're not good enough as you are but with the right direction you'll become better. Shit. I'm through being a goddam fool.

Trash: I know what you're talking about.

Garbage: (Talking to both but looking at Goodie Goodie) There's no use talking anymore. A person can't get anywhere. I was only trying to help. I really do care about you both though. I don't understand why you both come down so hard on me. (MEANING: A gross guilt trip. I'm a person and you're a couple of nobodies who aren't able to appreciate my superior help. You're to blame for your stupidity. You're on my shit list now and I'll think twice before I throw you a scrap of my approval. Aren't you sorry now for having behaved like you did when I really do care.)

Goodie Goodie: Help if you want to but don't expect me to jump when you bark. I'm not so sure if you do really care about us or if you only care about losing your power over us.

Trash: Well said sister.

Goodie Goodie: (To Trash) What would you think about going to a movie with someone as bad as me?

Trash: I wouldn't miss it for the world.